Worldwide Wonders

ANCIENT WONDERS

Clive Gifford

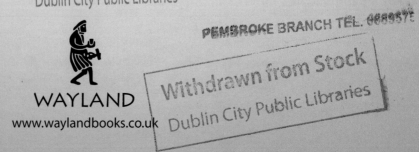

WAYLAND

www.waylandbooks.co.uk

Published in paperback in 2017 by Wayland

Editor: Nicola Edwards
Design: Peter Clayman

ISBN: 978 0 7502 9870 4
10 9 8 7 6 5 4 3 2 1

Wayland, an imprint of
Hachette Children's Group
Part of Hodder and Stoughton
Carmelite House
50 Victoria Embankment
London EC4Y 0DZ

An Hachette UK Company
www.hachette.co.uk
www.hachettechildrens.co.uk

Printed and bound in China

Picture acknowledgements: All images and graphic elements courtesy of
Shutterstock except p5b Wikimedia Commons, p7b NASA, p8t Getty images, p15b
Wikimedia Commons

Every attempt has been made to clear copyright. Should there be any inadvertent
omission, please apply to the publisher for rectification.

The website addresses (URLs) included in this book were valid at the time of
going to press. However, it is possible that contents or addresses may have
changed since the publication of this book. No responsibility for any such
changes can be accepted by either the author or the Publisher.

Contents

The Ancient Egyptian Pyramids

This book is all about the world's most amazing buildings and structures built by ancient civilisations centuries and centuries ago. Few are more ancient or inspire more wonder than the pyramids of ancient Egypt. The remains of over 110 have been found and the largest of all, built for Pharaoh Khufu, is more than 4,500 years old.

The four faces of the Great Pyramid (centre) align with North, South, East and West.

Giza Pleaser

The Pyramid of Khufu (also called the Great Pyramid of Giza) is huge – each side of its base measures 230.4m. A series of internal passageways and shafts leads to chambers inside, including the granite-lined King's Chamber where the pharaoh's body was laid to rest. At 146m high, it was the world's tallest building for more than 3,800 years until Lincoln Cathedral was built in the fourteenth century. Due to erosion and the loss of its outer facing stones and top capped stone, it now stands 138.5m high.

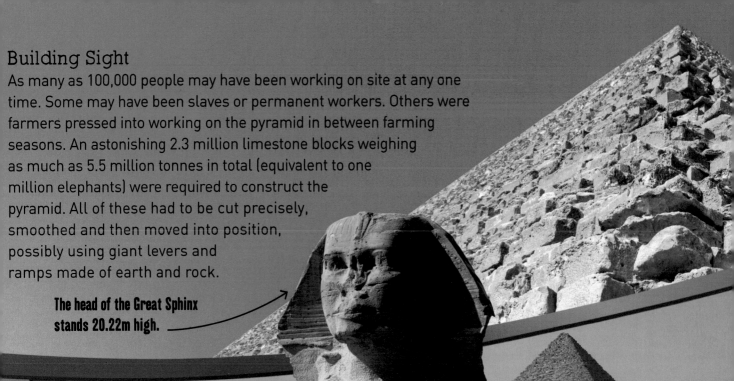

Building Sight

As many as 100,000 people may have been working on site at any one time. Some may have been slaves or permanent workers. Others were farmers pressed into working on the pyramid in between farming seasons. An astonishing 2.3 million limestone blocks weighing as much as 5.5 million tonnes in total (equivalent to one million elephants) were required to construct the pyramid. All of these had to be cut precisely, smoothed and then moved into position, possibly using giant levers and ramps made of earth and rock.

The head of the Great Sphinx stands 20.22m high.

Surrounding Structures

Khufu's Pyramid stands alongside a number of other ancient Egyptian monuments at Giza. These include the 136.4m-tall Pyramid Of Khafre, built for Khufu's son, as well as the Pyramid of Menkaere, smaller pyramids for members of Khufu's family, funerary temples and other tombs. The 73.5m-long Great Sphinx (above) – a massive and mysterious statue with the body of a lion and face of a woman – also stands nearby. All these wonders face threats from Cairo's urban sprawl which generates pollution that attacks the exterior stone. The stone blocks are also worn away by people climbing up them, even though this is forbidden.

WOW!

In 1954, a pit close to Khufu's Pyramid was found to contain 1,200 pieces of wood. These turned out to be a 43.6m-long barge (right), which made it the world's oldest intact ship. It is now on display in a building next to the pyramid.

Nazca Lines

Etched into the harsh Nazca Desert in Peru, some 320km away from the country's capital city of Lima, are an extraordinary series of lines, geometric patterns and giant images of people and creatures. These astonishing geoglyphs are only clearly viewable from the air or from the peaks of higher ground.

Mysterious collections of straight lines and patterns mark parts of the region.

Enduring Art

The desert stones and soil that cover the Nazca region are a dark red-brown colour. The Nazca people, who flourished in the region between around 200BCE and 600-700CE, found that removing the top 20-40cm of rock revealed a much lighter-coloured sand beneath (left). They used this knowledge to create vast numbers of lines over a 450km² area. With so little rain and relatively few winds in the region, the exposed designs can still be seen today.

The giant hummingbird with its long thin bil is one of several geoglyphs of birds, including the condor.

Desert Designs

No one is certain why the lines were produced. Some believe the lines map stars in the night sky, were used for ceremonies or were tributes to the Nazca people's gods. What is certain is that some of the designs are huge. The 70 or so artworks of nature include giant plants, trees and a hummingbird which measures approximately 50m, a 65m-long killer whale, a 46m spider and a monkey, the size of which at 93 x 58m is almost as big as a football pitch.

WOW!

Heavy windstorms in 2014 led to fears that the Nazca lines would be damaged. In fact, the winds blew away sand and dust to reveal more than 20 previously unseen geoglyphs, some depicting llamas.

The lines are clearly visible from the air.

Learning and Conserving

The lines became known throughout the world in the 1920s and 1930s when regular passenger air services in Peru began flying over the Nazca Desert. From 1946 to 1998, a German teacher named Maria Reiche devoted herself to learning about the lines and campaigning to preserve them. In 1997, the Nazca-Palpa Project was founded to conserve the lines, which received around 160,000 visitors in 2013. Vandalism, litter and large-scale graffiti (people etching their own messages in the land) threaten some of these ancient artworks.

Stonehenge

Britain's best-known ancient site, these giant standing stones on Salisbury Plain in the English county of Wiltshire developed over centuries of history to become Europe's most famous prehistoric monument.

Stone Circles

The first major construction at Stonehenge was a circular ditch, with banked areas built around 3100BCE. The giant stones began arriving around 2500BCE. The largest, weighing up to 50 tonnes, are sandstone blocks called sarsens, thought to have come from the Marlborough Downs, around 35km away. They may have been rolled to the site on large logs greased with animal fat. The sarsen stones were arranged in two rings, with the outer ring measuring approximately 33m across. The inner ring formed a horseshoe shape, made up of five trilithons (two vertical stones with a third lying on top) standing 6-7.3m tall.

Stonehenge viewed from the air shows the gaps in its circular layout.

Mysteries of Stonehenge

Stonehenge also contains smaller bluestones, which underwent a far longer and more mysterious journey. These stones are believed to have come from southwest Wales over 200km away, although no one is certain how they were transported. Debate also rages over Stonehenge's purpose. Different theories suggest that it was a site of human sacrifice, a healing centre, an astronomical calendar or a temple of worship. Large numbers of human remains excavated from more than 50 holes show that it was certainly used as a burial ground.

More than 80 remaining stones form the atmospheric stone circles which became a UN World Heritage site in 1986.

Conservation and Development

Some of Stonehenge's stones were stolen in the distant past, and today human impact from visitors and from heavily trafficked roads nearby is concerning conservationists. A new visitor centre opened in 2013, containing 250 ancient objects. Visitors are now taken the 2km from the visitor centre to the stones by shuttle bus. They are not allowed inside the stone circles but instead view them from a surrounding walkway. In 2014, 1.3 million people visited Stonehenge including US President Barack Obama.

WOW!

Stonehenge was sold at an auction in 1915 for £6,600. It was bought by lock-making businessman Cecil Chubb for his wife, but she didn't like it so he donated it to the nation three years later.

Angkor Wat

The city of Angkor in northwestern Cambodia was the centre of the Khmer Empire for over 500 years and Angkor Wat was the jewel in its crown. This magnificent collection of temples, buildings and sculptures was built in the twelfth century on the orders of Khmer ruler Suryavarman II as a Hindu place of worship, but later became sacred to followers of Buddhism.

Complex Layout

A large moat surrounds Angkor Wat which is crossed via a 188m-long bridge. The complex is enclosed by a 1,025m by 802m wall. This was constructed, like most of the complex, out of sandstone blocks which were quarried from more than 50km away and floated down the Siem Reap River on rafts. Inside the wall is a series of galleries, platforms and temples, culminating in four towers and a Central Sanctuary reached by steep steps.

Khmer Art and Apsaras

Beautiful stone sculptures and statues can be found throughout the temple complex, which also features over 1,200m² of stunning stone wall carvings depicting scenes of battles and gods from ancient Hindu epic stories. Angkor Wat is well known for its apsaras. There are more than 2,000 stone carvings of these female spirits found around the temple complex.

A pair of apsaras wearing headdresses dance in this stone wall carving at Angkor Wat.

The causeway crossing the giant moat is made from sandstone.

WOW!

According to inscriptions at the site, building Angkor Wat involved 300,000 workers and 6,000 elephants and took 6-10 million sandstone blocks, most weighing over a tonne!

Fall and Rise

Angkor was abandoned as a city after Thai armies invaded in 1431, although Angkor Wat remained a holy site to Buddhists. After centuries of disrepair, parts of the complex were restored and tourist numbers boomed from around 8,000 in 1993 to 2.35 million in 2014. With this huge increase comes threats from traffic pollution and wear and tear as tourists climb over and touch the stonework and wall carvings.

Tree roots dramatically obscure part of Ta Phonm temple at Angkor.

Teotihuacan

Located 50km north east of Mexico's present capital, Mexico City, Teotihuacan was founded around 200BCE. It became, at its peak around 450–500CE, the greatest city in the whole of North and South America. We know little about the people who built and lived in the city as there are no written records, but we can still experience the grandeur and art of the civilisation they left behind.

A City with a Citadel

At its peak, Teotihuacan covered an area of 20-30km^2 with a population possibly as large as 200,000. This may not sound a lot today, but at the time it would have made it one of the biggest cities in the world, bigger than Athens or Rome. Its layout appears to have been planned carefully, with a 40m-wide central street, called the Avenue of the Dead (below), running north-to-south some 2.4km through the middle. The city contained more than 2,000 apartment complexes, as well as workshops, temples, palaces believed to be inhabited by priests or nobles, and large squares and plazas. The largest plaza, about the size of 18 soccer pitches and surrounded by temples on all sides, is a sunken complex known as the citadel.

Pyramids of the Sun and Moon

The northern end of the Avenue of the Dead ends in the Pyramid of the Moon, the second biggest structure in the city. Located nearby is Teotihuacan's biggest building, the Pyramid of the Sun. It measures approximately 225m² and once stood as high as 75m, possibly with a temple at its top. A network of tunnels and chambers have been found underneath it.

Carvings at Teotihuacan include snakes and jaguars.

Visitors climb the 248 steps to the very top of the Pyramid of the Sun.

WOW!

In 2014, archaeologists found chambers underneath the Temple of Quetzalcóatl containing more than 50,000 objects including pottery and figures carved from jade – a real treasure trove!

Art in the City

Teotihuacan was attacked and burned to the ground, possibly in the seventh century, and many of its artworks were destroyed or stolen. The remaining pieces prove that the city contained remarkable artists and craftspeople. They produced striking stone masks using jade and greenstone, detailed stone sculptures of gods and creatures (above right) and complex pottery, as well as brightly-coloured murals which were painted on many walls.

The Colosseum

Masterful builders and engineers, the Romans constructed many extraordinary structures, few more astonishing than this gigantic 48.5m-tall amphitheatre. The largest stadium in the Roman world, it was capable of seating more than 50,000 spectators.

Almost five million people visit the Colosseum every year. Entry is free for EU citizens who are under 18 or over 65.

Complex Construction

Built on the orders of Roman Emperor Vespasian around 70-72CE, the Flavian Amphitheatre or Colosseum was an amazing feat of engineering. Drains were dug 8m below the structure to divert streams away from the doughnut-shaped foundations which were made of concrete. Above ground, the 189m x 156m building was made mostly from limestone blocks held together by almost 300 tonnes of iron clamps. The internal walls were made of brick and concrete.

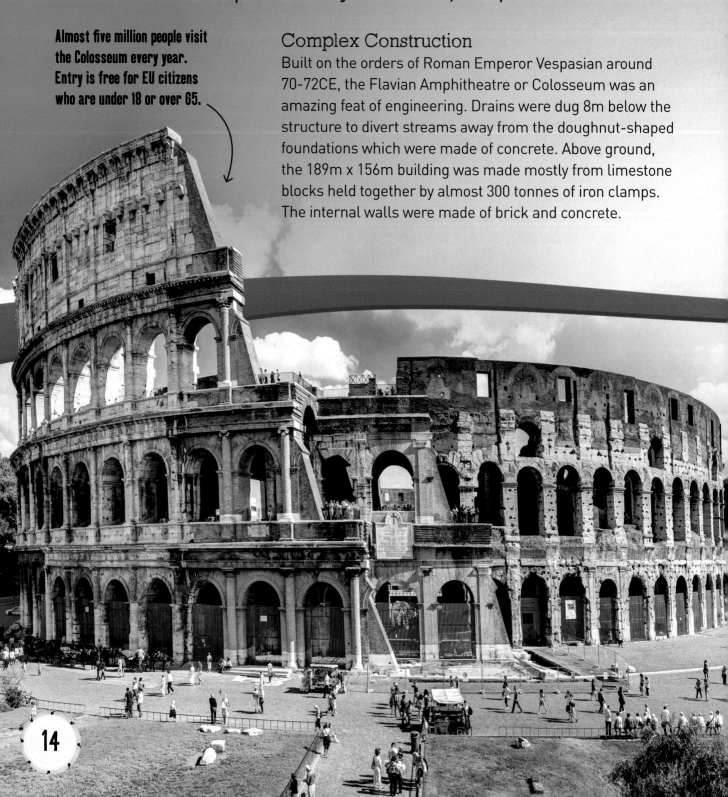

Awesome Architecture

At ground level, 80 entrance arches flanked by columns allowed visitors access into and out of the stadium. Passageways and staircases took them to their seats. The top levels were shielded from the sun by a giant awning called a velarium. The building's rows of arches piled on top of each other looked spectacular, especially as the outer face was once covered in sparkling travertine stone. After four centuries of use, though, the Colosseum was abandoned and this and other stonework was removed and used to build other structures including St Peter's Basilica.

WOW!

The Colosseum was opened in 80CE with 100 days of games in which over 9,000 wild animals, including rhinos, elephants and lions, were killed. Later events even included a mock naval battle with the arena flooded with water.

The striking interior of the Colosseum, the grandest of the Romans' 250 amphitheatres.

Thousands of gladiators fought and died in the Colosseum.

Gladiatorial Games

Opened in 80CE, the Colosseum staged ceremonies and criminal executions, but it is mostly known for its gladiatorial games. Slaves and criminals equipped with a variety of weapons fought wild animals or each other, sometimes to the death. These gladiators were trained in gladiator schools, the largest of which, the Ludus Magnus, was rediscovered in 1937 close to the Colosseum and linked to it by an underground tunnel. The Colosseum also contained vaults below ground level. These were used to hold scenery and wild animals which could be winched up in cages into the arena for battle.

The Great Wall of China

Built to keep invaders from the north out of China, the Great Wall is an enormous series of walls and barriers that, at their peak, totalled some 20.000km in length. Thousands of kilometres still exist and attract huge visitor numbers. During the week-long Chinese national holiday in October 2014 alone, as many as sixteen million people visited the Great Wall.

Paved stone walkways, often 4m wide, gave armies fast travelling routes through tough terrain.

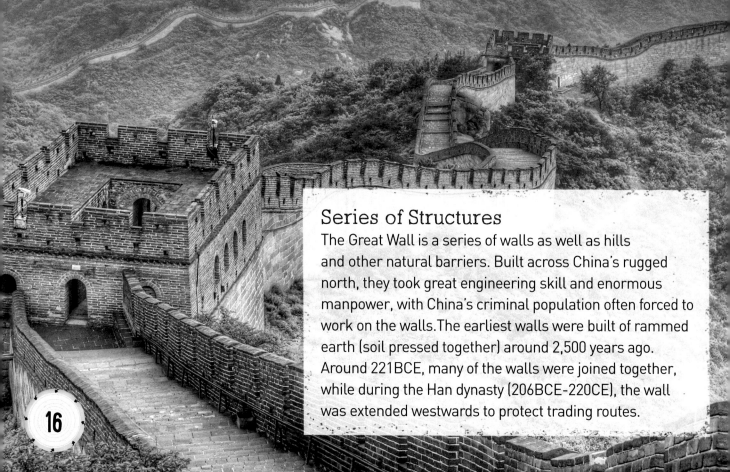

Series of Structures

The Great Wall is a series of walls as well as hills and other natural barriers. Built across China's rugged north, they took great engineering skill and enormous manpower, with China's criminal population often forced to work on the walls. The earliest walls were built of rammed earth (soil pressed together) around 2,500 years ago. Around 221BCE, many of the walls were joined together, while during the Han dynasty (206BCE-220CE), the wall was extended westwards to protect trading routes.

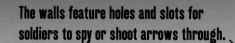
The walls feature holes and slots for soldiers to spy or shoot arrows through.

Mighty Ming

Between the fourteenth and seventeenth centuries, the emperors of the Ming dynasty embarked on a major upgrade of the walls, extending them greatly in length and using stone and bricks rather than rammed earth. Much of what remains of the Great Wall was constructed during this time, including hundreds of watch towers, mini stone forts which gave good views over the surrounding countryside. These were used as living quarters and storerooms and also as signal towers, ferrying messages along the wall using fires, flares or drums to communicate.

Under Threat

Many repairs and reconstructions to selected parts of the Great Wall took place in the twentieth century, although by then some parts of the walls had already been lost. Those parts that remain still face threats from crowds of visitors pounding the paved walkways (right), and from erosion due to rain and powerful sandstorms. In more isolated regions, stones from the wall are still taken by local people to sell or as building materials for their own homes.

WOW!

Researchers have found that a secret ingredient in the Great Wall's mortar used to cement its bricks and stones together was sticky rice. Substances in the rice made the mortar stronger and more water-resistant as a result!

Machu Picchu

In 1911, American explorer Hiram Bingham made a sensational discovery. Perched on top of a steep, narrow ridge and lying abandoned for four centuries, was a lost city of the Incas. Built in around 1450CE, Machu Picchu is one of the most spectacular archaeological sites in the world. surrounded by thick jungle and often shrouded in low clouds.

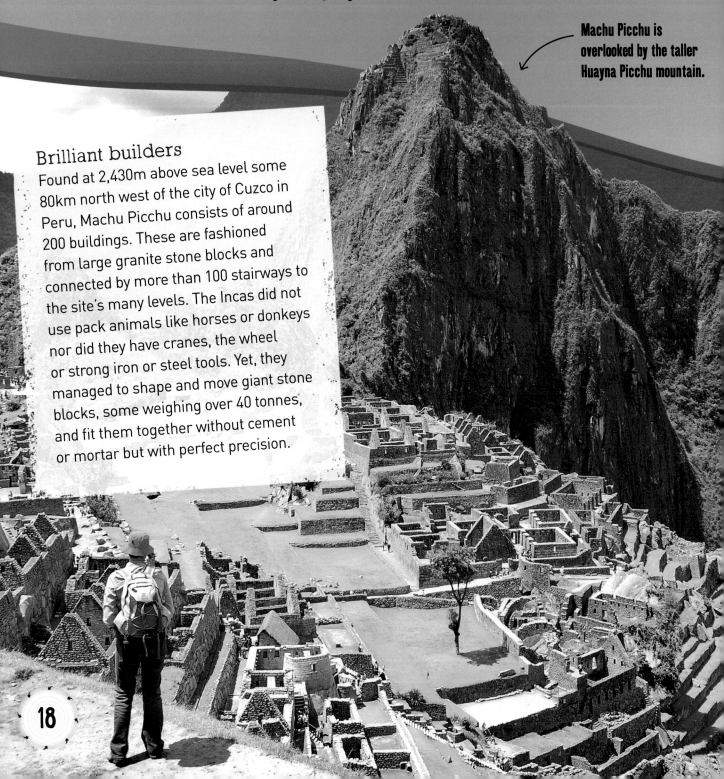

Machu Picchu is overlooked by the taller Huayna Picchu mountain.

Brilliant builders

Found at 2,430m above sea level some 80km north west of the city of Cuzco in Peru, Machu Picchu consists of around 200 buildings. These are fashioned from large granite stone blocks and connected by more than 100 stairways to the site's many levels. The Incas did not use pack animals like horses or donkeys nor did they have cranes, the wheel or strong iron or steel tools. Yet, they managed to shape and move giant stone blocks, some weighing over 40 tonnes, and fit them together without cement or mortar but with perfect precision.

Catching the rays

Machu Picchu is separated into different areas including residential and workplaces as well as palaces, large plazas and temples. One building, the Temple of the Sun, has windows positioned to capture the first rays of sunlight at solstices – the times of the year when the Sun is at its highest or lowest in the sky and causes the longest and shortest days of the year.

The Temple of the Sun is the only building in Machu Picchu to be circular-shaped.

The terraces at Machu Piccu look like the steps of a giant staircase.

WOW!

The sculpted Intihuatana stone is nicknamed, 'the hitching post of the Sun'. The corners of its carved rock pillar orientate towards the four major compass points and the stone was used as a solar calendar.

Steps to self-sufficiency

Terraces cut into the steep hillsides provided narrow strips of land to grow crops such as maize, potato and quinoa. This helped make the 1,000-1,500 people who lived in this isolated yet magnificent settlement self-sufficient. Water from natural springs and heavy rainfall was transported by a network of channels to provide fountains and irrigation for the crops.

Petra

Built more than 2,200 years ago as a city to serve trading routes, the stunning 'Rose City' located in present-day Jordan has captivated millions of visitors.

Cliff Carvings

The Nabataeans were an Arab people who built a large trading empire that extended through parts of present-day Jordan, Israel, Egypt, Syria and Saudi Arabia. Caravans made up of as many as 2,000 camels carrying spices, perfumes, precious metals and textiles travelled through the region regularly, paying the Nabataeans customs taxes and fees for using water holes. Over time, the Nabateans turned the water hole at Petra into a beautiful fortress city and major trading centre, hidden by giant colourful sandstone cliffs veined in red, orange, pink and purple. Petra's biggest buildings are carved out of these cliffs.

WOW!

Petra was forgotten and unknown to much of the world until Swiss explorer Johann Burckhardt. disguised as a Bedouin Arab. rediscovered the city in 1812.

The front façade of Al-Khazneh towers 43m high and is 30m wide.

A peak of Al-Khazneh can be seen from the narrow rocky alleyway of al-Siq.

Stunning Sight

Access to Petra is through a sharp 1.2km-long ravine called al-Siq. At points, this claustrophobic shaft is just 3m wide, with the ravine's walls towering 91-182m above. It opens out to give visitors a first amazing glimpse of Al-Khazneh (The Treasury), Petra's most photographed building, which may have served as a temple or major tomb. At its height, the city may have held 20,000 people. The remains of temples, streets and over 500 tombs chiselled into the rock remain, as well as a large amphitheatre seating up to 8,000 people and the Ad-Deir Monastery, which is reached by a flight of over 800 steps all cut into the rock.

Petra Threats

Petra has suffered from looting, earthquakes and floods in the past. Its elaborate and beautiful stone work and cliff carvings remain under threat from wind and water erosion as well as from the impact of thousands of visitors clambering over and touching its stonework. Motor vehicles are banned in Petra and climbing is now forbidden too. Park rangers help enforce rules to preserve the city.

Petra's giant amphitheatre contains 33 tiers of seats cut into the rock.

Easter Island

One of the most out of the way places on the planet, Easter Island lies some 3,500km from the coast of Chile in the south Pacific Ocean. This tiny, isolated island is populated with giant, brooding stone statues called moai which have excited and fascinated people for centuries.

Masses of Moai

A staggering 887 moai have been found all over the island. Many were moved over the rough, rocky ground from Rano Raraku to the island's coast. There they were placed upright on a long stone ceremonial platform called an ahu – an astonishingly tough task for the island's small population. Once on the ahu, some of the statues were decorated with a 2m-wide hair knot called a pukao. Carved out of red scoria stone, many of these were the weight of two elephants (around 11 tonnes) so raising them on top of the statue's head must have been another amazing feat of engineering.

WOW!

Found in Rano Raraku, the biggest moai, nicknamed El Gigante, would have stood 21m tall and weighed over 200 tonnes – more than an unloaded Boeing 747 airliner.

The largest ahu, Ahu Tongariki, has 15 statues.

Moody and Magnificent

The moai statues (left) are believed to have been carved from around the twelfth to late seventeenth centuries out of the rock of Rano Raraku, a volcanic crater. Each statue was sculpted out of the crater face using only primitive stone chisels as the Easter Islanders did not have metal tools. With their long, grave-looking faces, high foreheads and sloping noses, the moai look like no other statues on Earth. Most weigh many tonnes, while the tallest completed moai stands 9.8m high and tips the scales at 74.4 tonnes.

A completed moai with a topknot and eyes made of white coral with black obsidian in the centre.

History Mystery

Many mysteries surround Easter Island, from how the Polynesian peoples found and settled this tiny speck in the huge Pacific Ocean to why the statues were made and how they were transported and lifted. In addition, Easter Islanders had their own unique written script called rongorongo which no one today has been able to decipher. These mysteries and the atmospheric statues attract around 80,000 tourists to this small island each year.

The Alhambra

Breathtakingly beautiful, the Alhambra is a fortress and a palace all rolled into one. It was built on al-Sabika Hill overlooking the southern Spanish city of Granada. Its name comes from the Arabic for 'the red fort', referring to the reddish tint of its walls.

Changing Capitals

The Moors were Muslim peoples who invaded Spain from North Africa in 711CE. Conquering much of the Iberian Peninsula, they made the city of Cordoba their centre. In the thirteenth century, many Moors were driven out of Cordoba and fled to Granada, where they founded the Nasrid dynasty and built the Alhambra for their rulers. Work began in 1238 and the first section to be completed was the Alcazaba – a stout-walled fortress with towers and ramparts for defence. It was followed by the palace and the Upper Alhambra, a series of living quarters and chambers for the officials who helped run the kingdom.

WOW!

The Alhambra is located on a site around 740m long and 205m wide, packed full of buildings and courtyards.

French invaders turned the Alhambra into troop barracks and in 1812, destroyed several of the complex's towers. According to legend, whaen Napoleon ordered the entire Alhambra to be blown up, one soldier defused all the explosives to save the buildings.

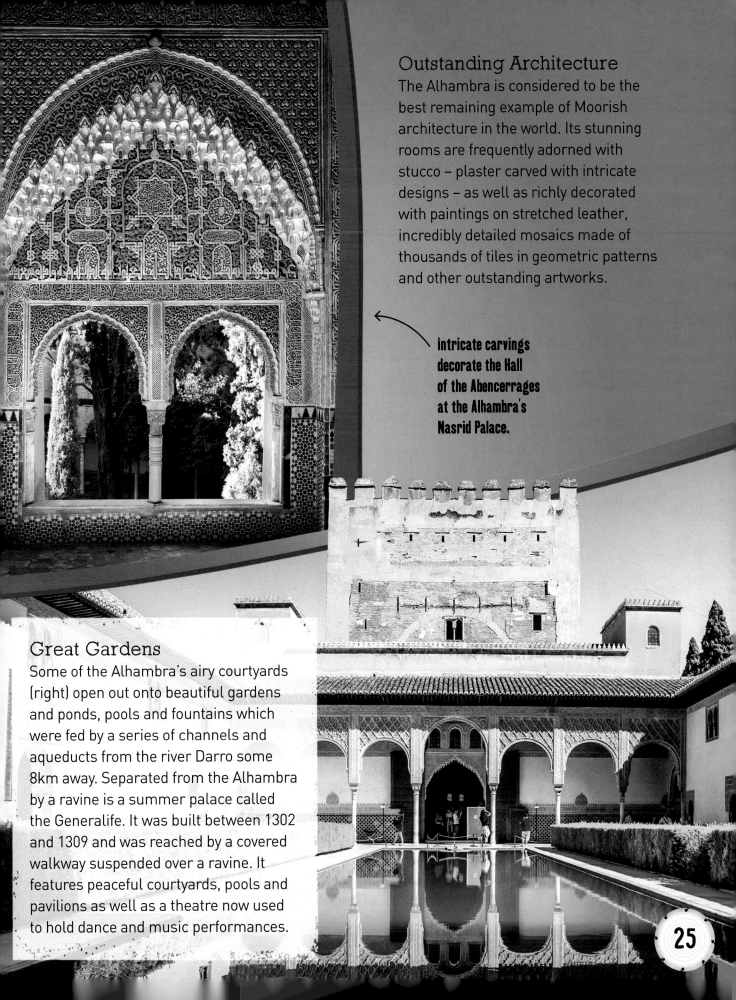

Outstanding Architecture

The Alhambra is considered to be the best remaining example of Moorish architecture in the world. Its stunning rooms are frequently adorned with stucco – plaster carved with intricate designs – as well as richly decorated with paintings on stretched leather, incredibly detailed mosaics made of thousands of tiles in geometric patterns and other outstanding artworks.

intricate carvings decorate the Hall of the Abencerrages at the Alhambra's Nasrid Palace.

Great Gardens

Some of the Alhambra's airy courtyards (right) open out onto beautiful gardens and ponds, pools and fountains which were fed by a series of channels and aqueducts from the river Darro some 8km away. Separated from the Alhambra by a ravine is a summer palace called the Generalife. It was built between 1302 and 1309 and was reached by a covered walkway suspended over a ravine. It features peaceful courtyards, pools and pavilions as well as a theatre now used to hold dance and music performances.

The Terracotta Army

In 1974, local farmers digging a well in the Chinese province of Shaanxi got a huge surprise when they broke into a giant pit. It contained not one or two life-size ancient figures sculpted out of terracotta clay, but a staggering 6,000 of them. Even more have been found in neighbouring pits, making it one of Asia's greatest ever archaeological finds.

The Tomb of an Emperor

Ying Zheng came to power in China in 246BCE and within 25 years he had brought together a number of warring kingdoms into one under his rule. He proclaimed himself the First Emperor of the Qin dynasty, by which time the work had already started on his giant tomb the size of a football pitch. The tomb was guarded from attack from the east by an enormous Terracotta Army numbering at least 8,000 warriors.

The terracotta soldiers are protected by this giant aircraft-hanger like building.

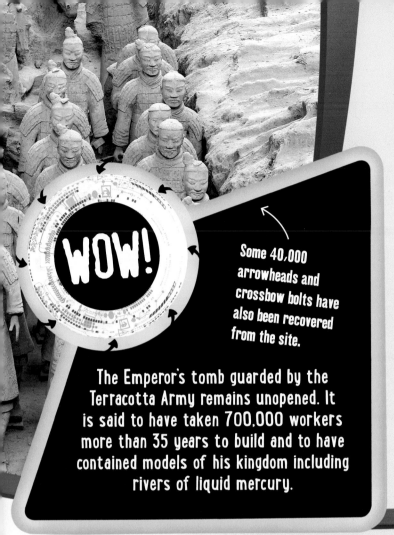

WOW!

Some 40,000 arrowheads and crossbow bolts have also been recovered from the site.

The Emperor's tomb guarded by the Terracotta Army remains unopened. It is said to have taken 700,000 workers more than 35 years to build and to have contained models of his kingdom including rivers of liquid mercury.

Amazing Individuals

The figures were cast in clay moulds but each figure has its own unique face. They were originally painted in bright colours which have faded over time. The figures are mostly foot soldiers, but there are also archers, chariots and horses as well as a group of army generals. For such a big undertaking, the amount of detail on each sculpture is extraordinary, with different uniforms, hairstyles and even a tread pattern on the sole of their shoes. Some held swords made of a special metal alloy of 13 substances which hasn't rusted despite being made over 2,200 years ago.

A high-ranking officer in a two layered tunic.

Terracotta Tour

The first pit to be discovered, approximately 230m long and 62m wide, was opened to the Chinese public in 1979. Four major pits have been excavated and are now covered and protected as part of a major museum which receives over two million visitors per year. Some of the figures have travelled long distances to be exhibited in the United States, Canada, Australia and Europe. In 2007, when 120 of the figures were exhibited at the British Museum in London for a few months, they attracted 850,000 visitors.

A four-horse battle chariot is one of the prize exhibits.

More Ancient Wonders

Astonishing ancient wonders exist on every continent, from majestic buildings and stunning artworks to magnificent cities.

Golden Wonder

Completed in 537CE in Constantinople (now Istanbul), the Hagia Sophia (Ayasofya in Turkish) was a Christian basilica until Ottoman ruler, Mehmed II conquered the city in 1453, when it became a mosque. Since 1935, it has been a museum, and attracted 3.57 million visitors in 2014. People come to see its majestic 32m-wide dome, its stunning collection of mosaics and sculptures and its golden interior covered in a staggering 30 million gold tiles.

Amazing Acropolis

A rocky plateau overlooking Athens was turned into a fortress by early Ancient Greeks. They later quarried dazzling white marble rock from Mount Pentelicus, 16km away, to construct incredibly beautiful temples, sanctuaries and statues. Chief amongst these is the majestic Parthenon, a temple built between 447 and 432BCE and dedicated to the ancient Greek god Athena. Measuring 70m long and 31m wide, with striking tall columns, the Parthenon is considered to be one of the finest examples of ancient Greek architecture.

The Parthenon featured eight giant columns at each end and 17 along its sides.

Tall towers called minarets stand 60m high.

Visitors can explore Bagan by horse and cart, taxi, on foot or using electric bikes.

Temple Town

The historic city of Bagan (formerly known as Pagan) in Myanmar was the scene of a temple building frenzy from around 1050CE, only halted by the invasion of Mongol armies in 1287. During that time, more than 10,000 beautiful temples, pagodas and other religious structures were built, many of which survive to this day.

Giant Buddha

Carved out of a cliff face around 1,300 years ago, the Leshan Giant Buddha is the tallest ancient stone statue. It stands 71m high and is so big that about 100 people could fit on one of its feet!

The statue has 28m-wide shoulders and 8.3m-long middle fingers.

Glossary and Further Information

amphitheatre
An oval or round building with rows of seats placed around an open area in the centre used for plays or in ancient Rome, bouts featuring gladiators.

apsaras
Female spirits in some religions, depicted at temple sites such as Angkor Wat.

aqueducts
A bridge or viaduct that carries a waterway over a valley or some other gap in the landscape.

basilica
A large church building in the Roman Catholic and Eastern Orthodox religions.

caravan
A group of people, often traders, travelling across a desert area, using mules, camels or other animals to carry cargo.

conservation
To preserve something to stop it being damaged or destroyed.

decipher
To decode or uncover the meaning of something, such as a code or ancient language.

dynasty
A line of rulers, usually related by birth, that lead a country, kingdom or territory.

erosion
The wearing away of surface rock and soil by wind, water and ice.

excavated
To remove earth and rocks or to dig carefully to try to find ancient objects at an archaeological site.

foundations
The lowest part of a building, which bears the weight of the rest of the structure.

geoglyphs
Large designs or pictures produced on the ground, usually by positioning rocks or removing surface rock and soil.

iconic
Describes a very famous and instantly recognisable image or symbol of something.

obsidian
A hard, glass-like volcanic rock.

pharaoh
A ruler of ancient Egypt.

pollution

Substances that contaminate the air, ground or water and make it harmful to some living things.

prehistoric

Describes a time in history before there were written records.

ramparts

A defensive wall often with a walkway along the top.

ravine

A deep and narrow gorge, usually with steep sides.

sediment

Matter such as sand, mud and pieces of stone that settle at the bottom of a liquid.

Books

The Land and the People: Mexico by Cath Senker (Wayland. 2016)

Visual Explorers: Wonders of the World by Paul Calver and Toby Reynolds (Franklin Watts. 2016)

Unpacked: China by Susie Brooks (Wayland. 2015)

The Best and Worst Jobs in Ancient Egypt by Clive Gifford (Wayland. 2015)

Website

https://www.tes.com/teaching-resource/building-the-great-pyramid-6174272
Watch this short clip from the BBC reconstructing how the Ancient Egyptians may have built Khufu's Pyramid.

http://www.aquiziam.com/ancient-mysteries/nazca-lines-google-earth/
View many of Nazca's most famous geoglyphs using Google Earth online.

http://www.the-colosseum.net/around/faq_en.htm
Almost every question you could possibly want to ask about the Colosseum is answered at this detailed website.

http://visitpetra.jo
See stunning panoramas and learn lots and lots about the fabulous ancient city of Petra at this website.

http://www.pbs.org/wgbh/nova/easter
Explore Easter Island's key sites and move a statue in this interactive minisite brought to you by PBS.

http://explorer360.org/peru/cusco/machu-picchu.html
Zoom in and move round stunning. full-screen 360° panoramas of Machu Picchu at this website. Click on the squares icon to pick different scenes of the ruined city.

http://ayasofyamuzesi.gov.tr/en/photo-gallery
Check out this great gallery of photos of the Hagia Sophia to see its wonders.

Index